IF YOU'RE READING THIS,
I DIDN'T GET INTO THE 27 CLUB

IF YOU'RE READING THIS,
I DIDN'T GET INTO THE 27 CLUB

a zine by **SJ CARL** (they/them)

Self-published in the United States of America

LIMITED PRINT RUN & E-BOOK RELEASED
MARCH 26, 2023

All cover & internal artwork by SJ Carl
Written by SJ Carl
Self-published by SJ Carl
sjcarlx@gmail.com

Co-edited by SJ Carl & Kayla Sutter

Author photo by Asad Esmail
Website: asadsphoto.com
Instagram: @asadsphoto

Paying homage to Rupi Kaur
inspiration (p. 118) from "home body" by Rupi Kaur

Excerpt from the film "Someone Great" written and directed
by Jennifer Kaytin Robinson
Governed by fair use.

Printed by Lightning Source, LLC in the United States of America

ISBN: 979-8-9879042-0-6 (Paperback)
ISBN: 979-8-9879042-1-3 (E-Book)

First Paperback Printing, 2023

Dedicated to Caitlyn Kovacs
Your spirit lives in all of us.
I choose to live.

CONTENT WARNING

This book explores themes around generational trauma, addiction, sexual assault, physical violence, abusive relationships, self-harm, and death. Readers who may be sensitive to these elements, please take note.

I want to thank best-selling poet, artist, and performer,
Rupi Kaur, for inspiring me to start writing again. Your words
helped me find strength, healing, and self-compassion in my own.

little poet
it seems like the more words you write
the more you think
it is you writing them
why do you think you're in control
didn't the words come spilling
out the first time
pouring without permission
and now you're trying to
make them work for you
but magic doesn't move like that
your rushing is
suffocating the masterpieces
baking inside you
your job is to
show up for the process
be patient and when it's time
the universe will use you again

inspiration - rupi kaur, home body (p.118)

Dear reader,

I started writing the poems in this book in May of 2018, and had originally planned for it to be an actual zine: photocopied and handmade, the whole nine yards. Over the years, it evolved in the most beautiful ways possible, and in 2023, became the poetry book you are holding in your hands. Nevertheless, in honor of my original vision, I will also be referring to this as a zine.

This zine was nearly 5 years in the making because writing about my mental health journey was not something I was willing to rush. It was very important for me to trust the process and write only when inspiration struck. But, as Rupi Kaur so perfectly wrote in her poem, *inspiration*, the universe has spoken, and the time has finally come to share my story with the world.

You may notice the usage of she/her pronouns throughout the zine, as well as references to myself as a cisgender woman. In 2022, I came out as gender-fluid and changed my pronouns to they/them. As many of the pieces within the collection were written prior to 2022, some pronouns have been adjusted where necessary. However, it was important to pay respect to, and recognize, the evolution that I've had throughout my journey.

This is not a suicide note, but rather a love letter. This collection tells (only a piece of) my story of trauma and healing. How I have become more resilient than I could have ever imagined, and how I learned to paint everlasting love for myself. And if you're reading this, I did just that. Even better, I made it to 28… I didn't get into the 27 club. But my story doesn't end here.

This book has changed my life, and I hope it changes yours, too. I will leave you with one question to ponder as you're reading my story: will **you** live, or simply exist?

xo,

v

TABLE OF CONTENTS

DEDICATION..i

CONTENT WARNING...iii

HOMAGE, *inspiration* by Rupi Kaur.........................iv

PROLOGUE...v

PART ONE: THE HURTING.................................1

    THE GREY 3

    THE BLOOMS 4

    IN POETRY WE SAY 5

    WHERE THE DEPRESSION COMES FROM............6

    THE BOYS WE KISS.......................................9

    FULL CIRCLE 13

PART TWO: THE HEALING 15

    MY LOVE SONG..17

    BURNOUT IS MY LIFELONG ADDICTION...........19

    BABY NAME GRAVEYARD..............................24

    TRAUMA HEALING IS NOT LINEAR 26

    IYKYK..28

    NEVERMORE...29

    QUOTE from the film *Someone Great*.....................30

    OUR SKY 31

    MY OWN BEST ADVOCATE 33

    PROTECT YOUR PEACE 34

    LOVE, SJ..35

WILL YOU LIVE, OR SIMPLY EXIST?....................37

ACKNOWLEDGEMENTS.....................................38

ABOUT THE AUTHOR 39

PART ONE:

The Hurting

1

if you're reading this, i didn't get into the 27 club

feeling lost
within myself
my heart and brain adrift
in their own disjointed realities
struggling to find my way
back
to where the thoughts and emotions
feel safe
i call it home

sj carl

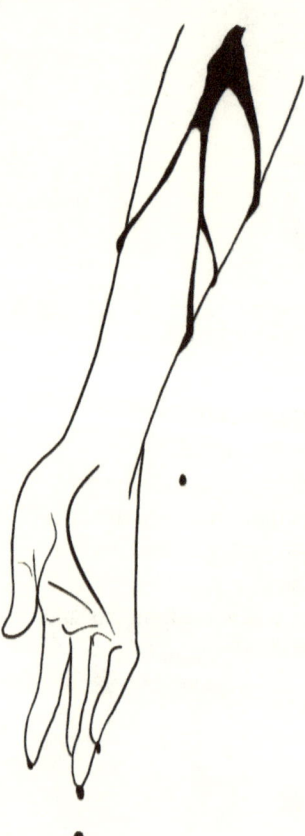

i was ready
for a life worth living
but i couldn't see
the light

the darkness
dragged me back
until it overwhelmed me
i was blinded

i was always prepared
for it to get worse
before it got better

if you're reading this, i didn't get into the 27 club

in english, we say
i'm anxious

in poetry, we say
i'm paralyzed as fear and overwhelm take over
my body gives in first
feet anchor to the core of mother earth
torquing open into the most powerful mountain i'm able to hold
the tension lives in my lockjaw
in my shaky, uneasy breath
in the knots that bore themselves deep into my shoulders
i am at the mercy of my own psychosomatic manifestations
a prisoner of my own mind

where the depression comes from

maybe i was born this way
maybe it's always been in my head
maybe it's an imbalance of three chemicals
that make me feel
sad even when i have nothing to be sad about
lonely even when i'm surrounded by people who love me
hopeless even when i have a bright future ahead of me
lazy even when i don't stop working
broken even when i'm the most put together i've been in years
maybe i was born this way

maybe it was because of my parents
maybe it came from the abuse of my mother
the bruises she left on my skin
on my heart
and on my mind
from the burden my siblings and i put on her
maybe it came from the neglect of my father
from my mother's abuse
maybe if he listened to my cries for help
for love
for a fucking childhood that was taken from me
maybe he thought if he ignored it all
it couldn't be real
maybe he couldn't fathom the thought
that he had failed me as a father
even now
maybe it was because of my parents

6

maybe i should have kept myself guarded
maybe that would have prevented
the barbed wire on my heart
and the knife in my back
from the men that never believed me
lied to me
and broke me
the men that promised love and protection with no intention
the men that taught me i was never going to be enough
the men that never deserved me
maybe i should have kept myself guarded

maybe it's all connected
the thoughts that constantly run through my head
telling myself i'm no good
the abuse and neglect from my parents
and the childhood i didn't have
the false love and protection that was taken away
as quickly as it was given
the scars on my heart
and the scars on my mind
maybe it's all connected

...or maybe it's just me

the boys we kiss

inching slowly
closer towards him
first my fingers
tip toeing to his fingers
one after the next
my heart beating faster
with every move i make
he makes
his heart beats too
as i feel our heartbeats aligning
my knees
move closer towards him
slowly enough
to barely even notice
but he notices
because we are infinite
in that moment

and the next second moves faster than the speed of light
our mouths pressed together
hungry like we haven't eaten in months
hands on places only some hands have permission
but his hands have permission…for now
undressing me with his eyes
as he takes off my clothes
lips and tongues moving from mouths
to other places
and baby we are moving

9

suddenly
fingers launch into me
like torpedos
and i am shocked
i do not like it
but i play so well
because baby this is what i'm used to
playing along on his terms
and never mine
i want to shout

    stop

      not like this

        you're hurting me

but i can't speak
so all i do is moan
like one of those girls
in the videos he watches
because baby
this is what i'm used to
and as quickly as it started
it is over
i hope it's over

he moves my mouth
towards a place i do not want to go
this time i say no
but he makes me go anyways
because this is what girls are taught to do
whatever that boy wants
whatever that boy needs
but never what we want
what we need
what we yearn for

no matter how many boys i have kissed
and done other things with
my pleasure is always on the back burner
next to his
never asking what i want
what i like
but doing what he sees
in the videos he watches
because that is what girls like, right?
wrong.

but how do we teach the boys we kiss
to ask us what we like
instead of doing what they think we like
how do we teach the boys we kiss
to respect us
to ask for consent
if we are taught from such a young age
that shrinking ourselves
is what boys like him want
and that knowing what we want
what we need
is not sexy
next to our obedience of him
how do we teach the boys we kiss
that we are just as important
as they are?

if you're reading this, i didn't get into the 27 club

rain drips down her face
as she spilt sour from her lips
the words stung him
like a needle drawing blood
and in that moment
she knew
she lost
what had made her
feel so good
the fire in her heart
was extinguished

PART 2:

The Healing

if you're reading this, i didn't get into the 27 club

i say i'm happy alone
but am i really?
because being alone means
you're no longer here to complete me
and i know…
i should be whole
on my own
never relying on you
to fulfill me
merely complement
like the chords to my melody
both independently complete

yet why does it feel so good
when you're the chorus to my song?
rather than the intro
that vanishes in the blink of an eye
why do i revive you in the bridge
when i know you won't always be here?
you proved that a long time ago
in a sudden key change
that threw my song out of tune

why can't i let go
of the chords that don't fit
in the composition
and write anew
i'll call it my love song

my love song will be my motivation
my love song will be my inspiration
my love song will be my innovation
and my love song will not be forsaken

17

sj carl

burnout is my lifelong addiction.

spring 2007, 12 y/o. the first cracks.

It started before I fully understood what mental health was. The trauma cracks that the pavement of my mental health endured during my childhood made room for the ADHD to germinate its seeds. However, as long as I was a subordinate to my routine, I was safe from myself. I convinced myself that I could achieve safety through perfection. I thought that if I was safe, the cracks would stop, and I could be happy. But that's the thing about weeds like trauma and ADHD, they're resilient and will choke out all available nutrients in order to sprout. Especially if the weeds are in their native environment.

you're being dramatic. pick up and keep going.

fall 2013, 18 y/o. major: burnout.

College was an unexplored meadow I was confronted with, and I didn't understand where my inherent skill for learning went. Everyone told me that I would eventually adjust, that it would get easier. Yet, the academic adjustment never seemed to come, and the seedlings of my ADHD grew stronger. I was soon so intoxicated by its beauty that I could no longer resist, and I went all in with no regard for the further impact the weeds would have on my pavement.

pick up and keep going. make it happen like you always have.

19

fall 2014, 19 y/o. the first bloom: burnout, meet breakdown.

The cracks continued to spread as the weeds finally consumed all of the nutrients I had to give. It was finally too much to handle and the first bloom burst out of me, taking over my mind and body. Yet, I was still convinced that I needed to be perfect, even though I knew that was an impossible standard to live up to: plants cannot thrive in a nutrient-deficient environment. In an effort to repair my pavement, I started therapy and took academic sabbatical.

force reset…but not for too long. pick up and keep going.

winter 2015, 19 y/o. spring semester: who am I?

Craving that feeling of safety, I ran to the version of myself that I thought I needed to be. To be successful and provide for myself, so I could be happy just like the other beautiful flowers in the meadow. I never knew this was masking; I didn't even know what masking was. It never occurred to me that nature didn't work like that, life doesn't work like that. You can't go through life pretending to be someone you're not, and still expect to be fulfilled. I constantly tried to replace my classes with my extracurriculars because I still couldn't say no to ADHD's intoxication. It felt too good to follow my passions, to give in to the weeds and feed my addiction. The burnout lingered and the cracks continued to grow.

pick up and keep going. make it work. you have no choice.

spring 2018, 23 y/o. the second bloom: keep going, they said.

College was ending, and I thought I'd finally solved the meadow's puzzle. After the first bloom, I acquired a pair of pruning shears and started medication for my depression, so I could keep myself free of weeds. I would be prepared for the next bloom. As I worked to repair the last of the cracks in my pavement, the ADHD blooms were finally identified. I started taking medication that would help me prune the weeds as they sprouted through my pavement. That was the start of the second bloom. This time, the blooms took shape in the form of a break-up with my addict ex-fiancé & my rape on graduation night. I pruned these blooms in the poems I wrote in the formation of this book. I thought I finally figured it out, I thought the bloom was over. I didn't know how wrong I was.

pick up and keep going. force reset is not an option.

summer 2019, 24 y/o. career: burnout

I thought if I kept trying to be perfect, I would be safe. I could prevent the blooms from coming back. I didn't have to like my job because one day, I *would* have a job I loved. "It'll happen soon, don't worry!" everyone said. But, it never happened. I started to live in this cycle of burnout, it was my addiction. No matter how long it was gone, it always came back because it was my best friend. It was who I was. The blooms were too intoxicating; the highs and lows were exhilarating. But, that's the addiction talking. I couldn't afford to see my doctors so I had to stop taking my medication. My shears broke and I couldn't stop the weeds from growing. I couldn't stop the cracks. And when I couldn't stop the blooms from happening, I went on my death tour, and I consumed every drop of nutrition out of my last love: music, to feed them.

pick up and keep going. force reset is still not an option.

spring 2020, 25 y/o. the bloom continues: the pandemic.

The career burnout persevered, and the weeds continued to grow stronger. My pruning shears had been broken for so long, and I couldn't find a new pair as hard as I tried. Eventually, the blooms started to suffocate me, so I started seeing my doctors again in an effort to keep myself safe. But all I could think about was being a flower in a graveyard. Death had such a sweet taste. Its poison was intoxicating, and I started to crave it.

meet SJ.

summer 2021, 26 y/o. the second bloom: the finale.

I couldn't take it anymore. The blooms finally became too overwhelming and broke me. The finale was just as toxic as the first bloom in 2014. Therapy wasn't enough anymore and I could no longer sustain the habitual career burnout…meet breakdown. I'd convinced myself for the past year that if I could just get back on my ADHD medication, I could get through it, and my craving for death would finally go away. That I would finally get a new pair of pruning shears to stop the weeds from turning my pavement to rubble. But no doctor would help me, so the weeds bloomed into a beautiful garden of wildflowers. Force reset. I found a new job and was excited for the possibility that I could finally start my dream career there…eventually. I'd be able to finally germinate the seeds of my passion. I would be safe and stop the cracks. I could finally be happy.

pick up and keep going. make it happen like you always have.

winter 2023, 27 y/o. the third bloom: a new perspective.

I got new shears after years of searching and I was convinced that I was finally safe. In the time since the second bloom, I stopped masking and finally knew who I was. But, I got too comfortable and let my guard down. I forgot, that's the funny thing about weeds; they're resilient. They sneak up on you and slowly deplete you of all your nutrients. I was trying so hard to be perfect, for too long. Still holding myself to the same impossible standards I'd always been convinced would finally make me happy & fulfilled. Even though I was back in regular therapy and on medication to help control the weeds of my ADHD, the third bloom snuck up on me. But this time, I finally realized where my thinking went wrong all these years. I accepted that my pavement would never be smooth, the blooms would always be a possibility. While I might never fully end this addiction, I knew I had to accept my environment in order to grow. I had to start trusting myself. The trauma and triggers will always be there, and I might never feel 100% safe. But as long as I let the blooms control me, I'll never grow. I'll never blossom on my own if I keep growing gardens out of my weeds.

have the courage of your convictions, SJ.

march 26, 2023, 28 y/o. IF YOU'RE READING THIS, I DIDN'T GET INTO THE 27 CLUB.

Happy birthday to us, we've made it. I can finally hold you in my hands and feel proud of far I've come. While I understand this journey will never fully end, I am finding peace and closure in my own resilience. In my ability to grow and control my own garden, with disinterest in anyone else's perception of it. I am accepting this sign from the universe that the story of my journey is ready to be shared with the world. I finally believe in myself.

I am taking control back.

I used to think I wanted kids because society told me I should. That I would be happy if I lived in a house with a white picket fence in the suburbs with my husband and children. So, I started collecting these names when I was just a kid myself. They travelled with me through sticky notes on my childhood bedroom walls, scribbled in random notebooks that got lost and then found years later, and in the notes app of every cellphone I've ever had.

But the problem is, I'm not her anymore. I learned who I was, and what I wanted. I burned down the perfect house in the suburbs and knocked down that fucking picket fence. I kicked out the fiancé who was too afraid to touch me, who disrespected and lied to me. I gave myself the gift of sterilization despite politicians overturning Roe, so it would be impossible for me to become pregnant if I was ever raped again.

Because now, **I decide what comes next for me.** So, welcome to my baby name graveyard.

trauma healing is not linear.

Trauma creates triggers, and when we're triggered, we're provided the opportunity to rework the associated trauma. In time and with practice, our triggers can become less scary. This process looks different for everyone, but to me it has meant creating healthier boundaries that will help me improve my trauma response when I am met with a trigger. Just like any other muscle, the more you use it, the stronger it will become.

Addiction was my first trigger. My egg donor has always been an addict of all trades, but a master of alcohol and drugs. Her addictions sparked my traumatic childhood and activated this specific trigger. I had my first taste of what an abusive relationship looked like, and my trust issues became actualized. In response, I became emotionally avoidant.

I started therapy in college and created the boundary that I would maintain distance from those actively struggling with addiction. I was in a relationship and eventually got engaged. In 2018, it was revealed that my partner was an addict. I was heavily triggered by the sudden onset of his abusive behaviors caused by addiction that came out of nowhere. In response, I enforced my boundary. My cat Gandalf & I left to start the rest of our lives, and while continuing my mental health journey, I started writing this zine.

At my 2022 corporate holiday party, I discovered the woman I was seeing was an alcoholic in need of her own healing. She suddenly became a danger to herself and others. While I was triggered by these behaviors, I was also able to compartmentalize my trigger, deescalate the situation, and get her home safely. Afterwards, I reinforced my boundary and used this traumatic experience to rework my childhood trauma response to addiction.

While addiction was my first trigger, it was far from my last. Not all triggers are created equally, so it's crucial to understand what yours are and how they affect you. Healing from trauma will never be linear, and it requires motivation to do the self-work necessary to continually re-process your past trauma and the triggers which they've created. There will be good days, but there will also be bad days. But, if you put in the work, the bad days will eventually be few and far between. Continue to flex that muscle - it will eventually become something you don't even realize you're doing.

Always remember, it's okay not to be okay. When you become triggered, take a deep breath and realign your breath. Focus on the present and hydrate. Feel the emotions, and then use them to rework your trauma; the memories cannot hurt you if you don't give them the power to. This is a lifelong journey, and your trauma response will constantly evolve.

Do not try to fully get rid of your emotions, as learning how to experience them and turn that energy into fuel is a very powerful skill that will further your growth. I used to think my emotions were too strong, and that I felt too much. But that was just the world telling me to be quiet, and I'm so glad I didn't listen. Because if I did, I wouldn't be who I am today. I wouldn't be here telling you my story. So, take a deep breath in and out. Prioritize your mental health and whatever you do, continue to be your own best advocate, because no one will rally behind you like you do.

There's a little secret I learned to figuring out if someone actually wants to be in your life: IYKYK. And if you're confused, there's your answer. It's as simple as that.

if you're reading this, i didn't get into the 27 club

i'm concerned about you
she peers through the lens of someone who lives in delusion
her kaleidoscope vision distorting her reality
alleging to be a mental health advocate
though she is more reminiscent of a keyboard warrior

you're acting out
she is fanatical about the irrelevant
yet indifferent about the significant
as if embellishing my blank canvas in captivating artwork
is somehow abuse
and showing it unconditional love
is somehow in spite of its beauty
quite the oxymoron

i'm not gaslighting you
she is ignorant to the implications of her words
emboldened by the thought of being righteous
yet oblivious that it is actually doing me a disservice
she has failed to impose the pygmalion effect

i know i'm not a good friend
my endeavors to eradicate miscommunication are in vain
when the pages turn and stick to each other
i am ostracized when i am my own best advocate
but i am no longer willing to be belittled
for moving on is imperative

if you need me, i will be here
superficial at its core, our relationship was ephemeral
nevermore will i turn a blind eye
to red flags and narcissistic behavior
i am finding closure in wax poetic
i am finding peace right where she left me

29

Do you think I can have one more kiss? I'll find closure on your lips and then I'll go. Maybe, also, one more breakfast, one more lunch, and one more dinner. I'll be full and happy and we can part. But, in between meals, maybe we can lie in bed one more time? One more prolonged moment where time suspends indefinitely as I rest my head on your chest. MY hope is if we add up the one more's, they will equal a lifetime. And I'll never have to get to the part where I let you go. But that's not real, is it? There are no more 'one mores.' I met you when everything was new and exciting, and the possibilities of the world seemed endless. And they still are. For you. For me. But not for us. Somewhere between then and now, here and there – I guess we didn't just grow apart...we grew UP. When something b r e a k s, if the pieces are large enough, you can fix it. Unfortunately, sometimes things don't break. They s h a t t e r. But when you let the light in, shattered glass will glitter. And in those moments – when the pieces of what we were catch the sun – I'll remember just how beautiful it was. Just how beautiful it will always be. Because it was us. And we were magic. Forever.

-Excerpt from the film *Someone Great*

the sky glows pink
as bright as fire
the cloud's smoke burns
through the heavens
the sun glitters gold
as radiant as my everlasting love
for you
the moon watches over
like a guardian angel

for i've never seen
such a breathtaking view
do you see it too?

whenever i am missing us
i remember
we share the same sky so
you will always be out there
somewhere
looking up

and when i feel alone in this world
i look up
at the sky we share
and i am reminded
of how grateful i am
that loving you
showed me
how much more
i could love myself

if you're reading this, i didn't get into the 27 club

i want to thank you
for helping me grow
for i have learned to love myself more ferociously
than i ever knew possible

i want to thank you
for the compassion you gave me
for you have shown me that i deserve the patience and love
i thought i was never worthy of

i want to thank you
for restoring my faith in others
i have not forgotten how scary this world can be
but you, my dear
you have helped me bring the color back to my achromatic vision
i used to see the world in rose-colored glasses
but recently it's been washed out
i forgot how beautiful cotton candy clouds can be
how the sun paints the sky
in a sea of luminous pigment every night

i want to thank you
for reminding me life can be worth living
and even though you may no longer be in mine
i am grateful for the spot you once held
for you showed me nothing but unwavering support
even though i never asked for it

i want to thank you
for reminding me how i used to paint love for myself
over the scars i carved in my skin and on my heart

so thank you
for impelling me to be my own best advocate

Take life one day at a time. When one day is too long, because
life can certainly be that way sometimes, take it one moment at a
time. And if all else fails, and even a singular moment is too
much, take a nap… Prioritize your mental health and physical
well-being. I promise it will all be worth it in the end.
You are more important than all of the noise that surrounds you.

silky scarlet lace kisses their skin
as they slip into their best lingerie
fingers sensually gliding up their thighs
caressing their hips
gently nuzzling their breasts
it glows bright like fire
almost too vivid
against their fair skin

they're mesmerized
by the ocean eyes of the belle in the mirror
seeing pain crack
through her tender exterior
she is bittersweet and tortured
heart-breaking beauty
they recognize
that while she is bruised
she is not broken
she is vulnerable
yet she possesses unimaginable strength
come hell or high water
she is learning more each and every day
how building up her trust and self-worth
is the greatest gift
she can give herself

i am the belle i see in the mirror
i am the resilience i see in her eyes
i am the lust i have for myself
i am the love of my own life

35

will you LIVE,
or simply EXIST?

Thank you for reading.
Now, I challenge **you** to live.
Don't just exist.

ACKNOWLEDGEMENTS

Thank you to everyone who's bought this book, it's a dream come true
to be able to share this with the world.
Thank you Gandalf, you are the most important person in my world,
forever. I would not know me, if I didn't have you. Thank you for
showing me what it means to truly love without inhibition. It will hurt
to lose you, but I am a better person for having you in my life.
Thank you Sam, not many people know me as well as you do, or have
experienced this journey with me like you have. I will forever be
grateful to have such a loving and passionate friend as you in my life.
Thank you Cort, you're an amazing friend with such a big heart. You
have helped me grow so much just by being you. Love you endlessly.
Thank you Aaron, for being my cheerleader & confidante. There's no
one I've talked to more about this book than you. You're always
listening & letting me talk your ear off. Grateful to have you in my life.
Thank you Alyea, you were such a wonder mentor and have always
inspired me to shoot for the stars. Well, I did. And now, I'll never stop.
Thank you to the rest of my LEL pro staff, Ryan, Jordan & Robyn. I'll
never forget my roots or stop working to leave my mark on the world.
Thank you Kayla for being my co-editor! Grateful for you, my friend.
Thank you Gram, you have been the #1 supporter of my art for my
entire life, cheering me on. For that, I am indebted to you. Ily2, Gpa.
Thank you Caitlyn, you inspire me every day to be stronger.
I promise I will always choose to live. One day we'll meet again.
Thank you Asad, you are so genuine…and also an incredible photog!
Thank you to everyone who has supported me throughout this journey:
Laur, Jay, Mack, Allison, Ben, Luke, Eric, Liana, Jacq, Dan, Stuart,
Nikki, Tim, Ty, Jess, Erica, Bren, Mabs…missing some, but love y'all.
Thank you to my EMBRACE fam, you empower me every single day.
Thank you Ida, you've witnessed so much of this journey and helped
me grow so much. I think you would be proud of where I am today.
Thank you Bonnie, you have helped me so much in such a short time.
I am excited to keep working together and further grow on my journey.
Thank you Carey, you were the first person to ever support me in my
mental health journey. I don't know where I would be if you hadn't.
Thank you Magic Giant for it all, forever celebrating the reckless!
Thank you Rupi, your poetry inspired me to start writing again.
Thank you to Taylor Swift, Movements, Trash Boat, Noah Kahan, Real
Friends, Scene Queen, Microwave, Mayday Parade, The Wonder
Years, and Halsey. Your music's helped me get through the thick of it.

38

ABOUT THE AUTHOR

SJ Carl (they/them) is a passionate queer & gender-fluid artist, writer, and activist. They graduated from Rutgers University New Brunswick in 2018, earning a Bachelor's degree in Communications with a specialization in Organizational and Community Leadership & a minor in Entrepreneurship from Rutgers Business School. SJ is a multifaceted creative with professional experience in marketing, communications, event coordination, management, music-entertainment, hospitality, and sales. They are proud to be the Chair of the Board of EMBRACE, their company's Employee Resource Group that supports the LGBTQIA+ community and allies. When SJ is not working or flexing their creative muscles, they enjoy cuddling with their cat Gandalf, spending time at the Jersey Shore, being outdoors with friends, and enjoying live music. **IF YOU'RE READING THIS, I DIDN'T GET INTO THE 27 CLUB** is their first book. Connect with SJ on social media.

Instagram: @_sjayy__
LinkedIn: www.LinkedIn.com/sjcarl1
Email: sjcarlx@gmail.com